Cello Time Jog

a first book of very easy pieces for cello

Kathy and David Blackwell

Illustrations by Alan Rowe

Welcome to the Second Edition of **Cello Time Joggers**. You'll find:

- open string pieces and tunes using the finger pattern 0-1-34
- duets—start with the staves marked ☆; come back and play the other part later
- one new piece, replacing no. 3
- audio play-along tracks for all pieces (including scales and Super Sprinter exercises) available to download from www.oup.com/ctjoggers2e or to access on principal streaming platforms
- scales and arpeggios in the keys of G, D, and C major, one octave
- piano and cello accompaniments available separately in printed collections
- An ideal book to use alongside *Cello Time Starters*

OXFORD
UNIVERSITY PRESS

1. Bow down, O Belinda

American folk tune

Printed in Great Britain

OXFORD UNIVERSITY PRESS, MUSIC DEPARTMENT, GREAT CLARENDON STREET, OXFORD OX2 6DP

2. Under arrest!

KB & DB

Count 2 bars

pizz.
Four short crot-chets played on G, (rest) one fell off and left just three. (rest)
Four short quar-ter - notes on G,
7
1 2 3, (rest) 1 2 3, (rest) one fell off and left just three. (rest)

Say the word '*rest*' quietly to yourself as you play.

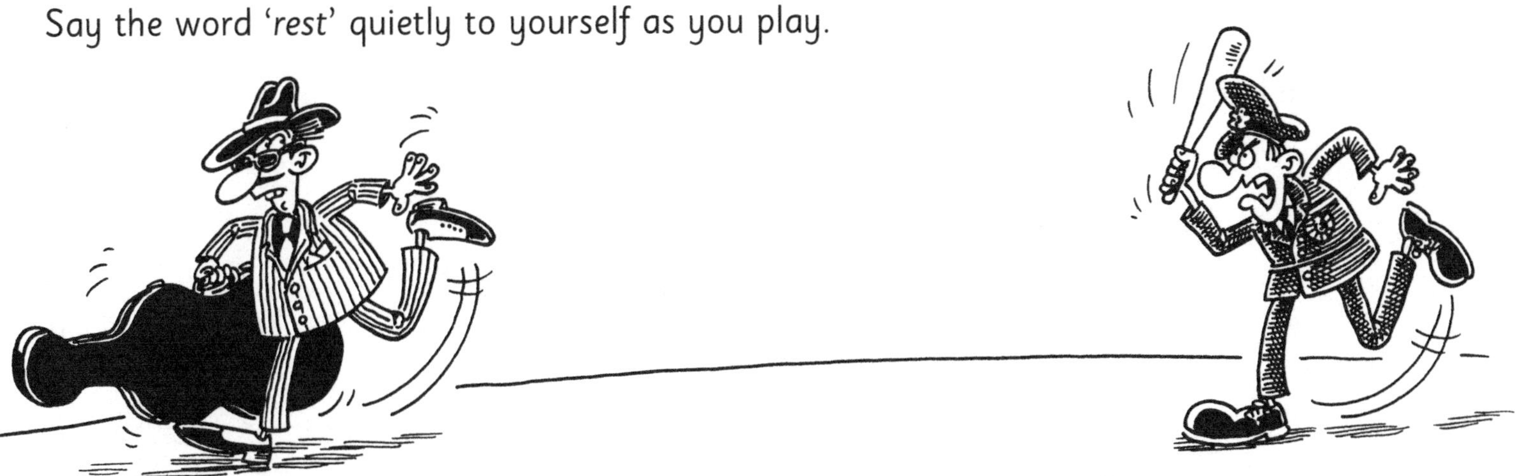

3. Someone plucks, someone bows

Traditional
Words KB & DB

pizz.
arco
Down, up goes the bow, when we're play - ing fast or slow;
3
down, up goes the bow, when we're play - ing high or low.

4. Down up

KB & DB

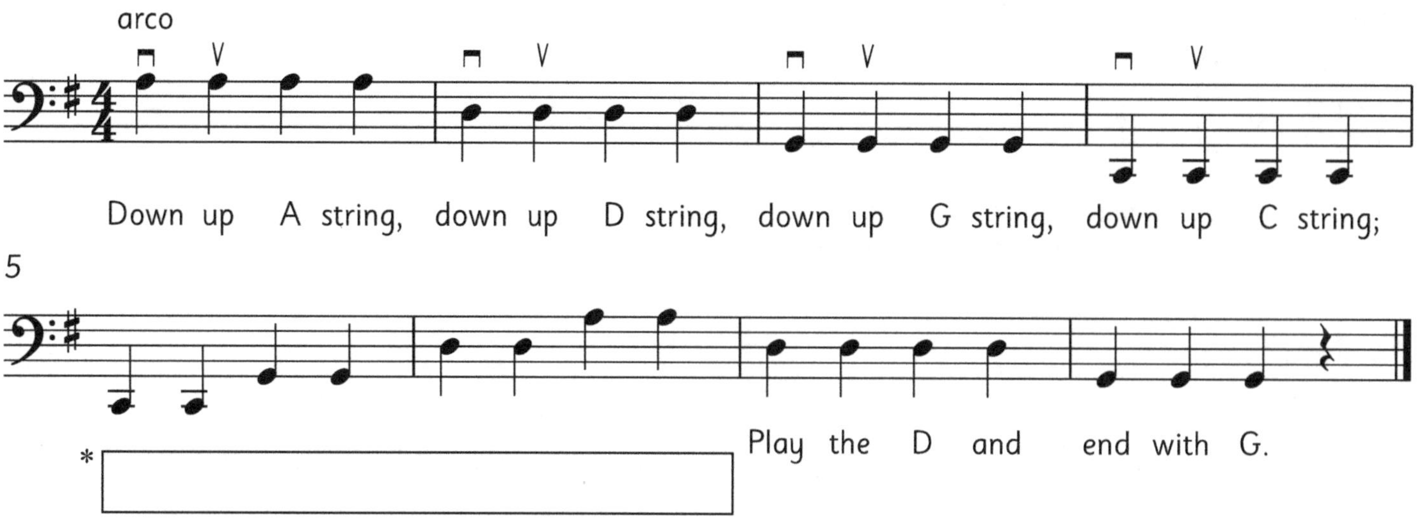
arco
Down up A string, down up D string, down up G string, down up C string;
5
Play the D and end with G.
*

* Fill in the letter names of these notes.

5. Hill an' gully rider

Trad. Jamaican

5

6. Fast lane

KB & DB

Try even faster the second time through!

7. In flight

KB & DB

In the rests, let your bow make a circle as you swoop and soar like a bird.

8. Lift off!

Rock

KB & DB

Lift your bow off in each of the rests and let it orbit! (Make a circle with your right arm.)

Rhythm game:

Or - bit round the moon. *(etc.)*

9. Katie's waltz

Count 4 bars

KB & DB

Gently

1st Finger
0 1
C D
0 1
G A
0 1
D E
0 1
A B
semibreve
(whole-note)
semibreve rest
(whole-note rest)

10. Copy cat

KB & DB

1
G G A A
Can you play what I play? G G A A
5
Fine
Can you play what I play? Play it now with me.
9
1
D D E E
Can you play what I play? D D E E
13
D.C. al Fine
Can you play what I play? Play it now with me.

11. Rhythm fever

Count 2 bars

KB & DB

Rock tempo

7
12
16
Rhy-thm fe - ver, 1 2 3 4 feel the beat, 1 2 3 4
feel the rhy-thm, 1 2 3 4 in your feet. 1 2 3 4 Feel the rhy-thm
as you play it, feel the beat go 1 2 3 4 Rhy-thm fe - ver,
1 2 3 4 rhy-thm fe-ver, 1 2 3 4 rhy-thm fe-ver, oh yeah!

12. Here it comes!

KB & DB

1
Through the teeth and past the gums, so watch out, tum-my, here it comes!
5
*
9
Through the teeth and past the gums, so watch out, tum-my, here it comes!

* Think of a foody rhythm and play it on these notes.

Here is an idea to start you off:

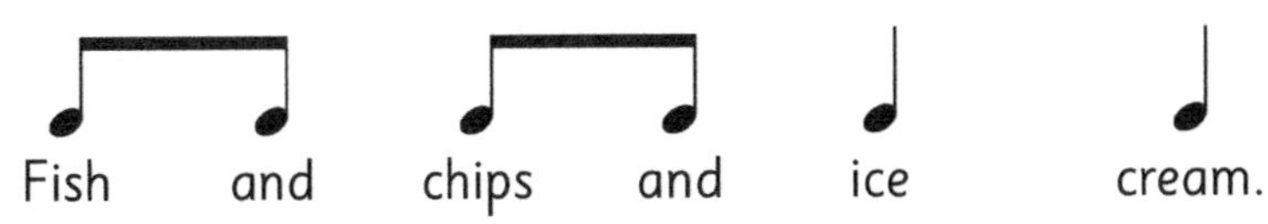
Fish and chips and ice cream.

13. Tap dancer

KB & DB

* Tap the cello with your left-hand fingers.

14. So there!

Count 4 bars

KB & DB

15. Rowing boat

KB & DB

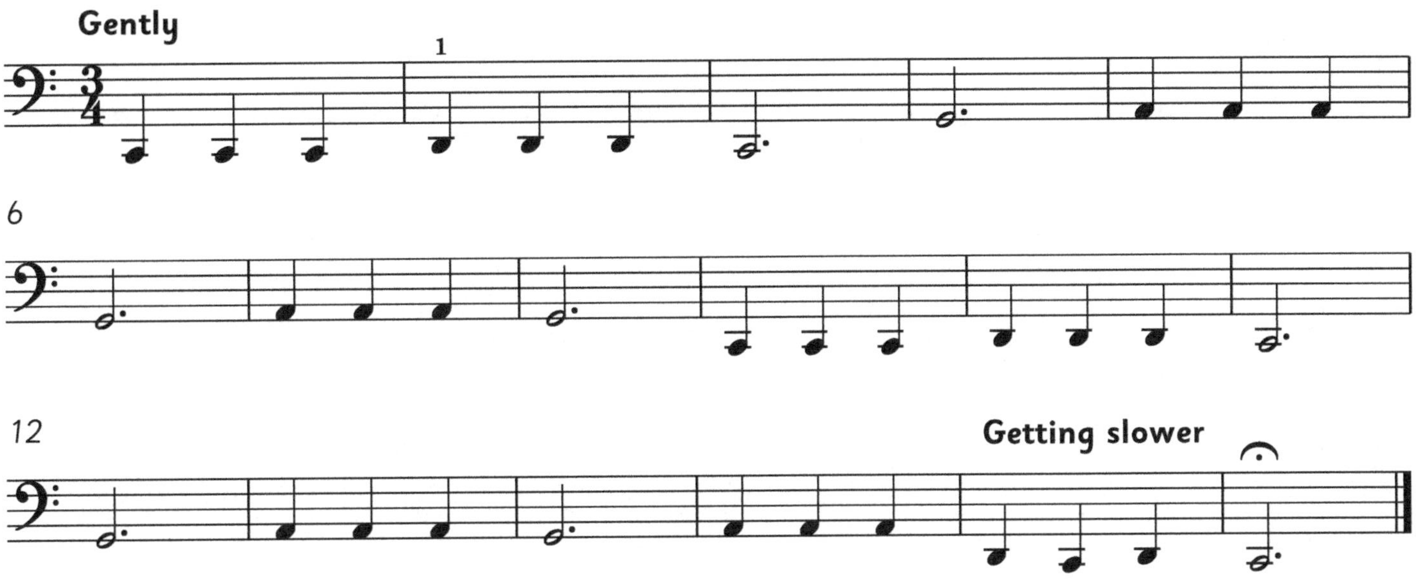

16. Ally bally

Scottish folk tune

17. C string boogie

KB & DB

* Be careful!

18. Travellin' slow

KB & DB

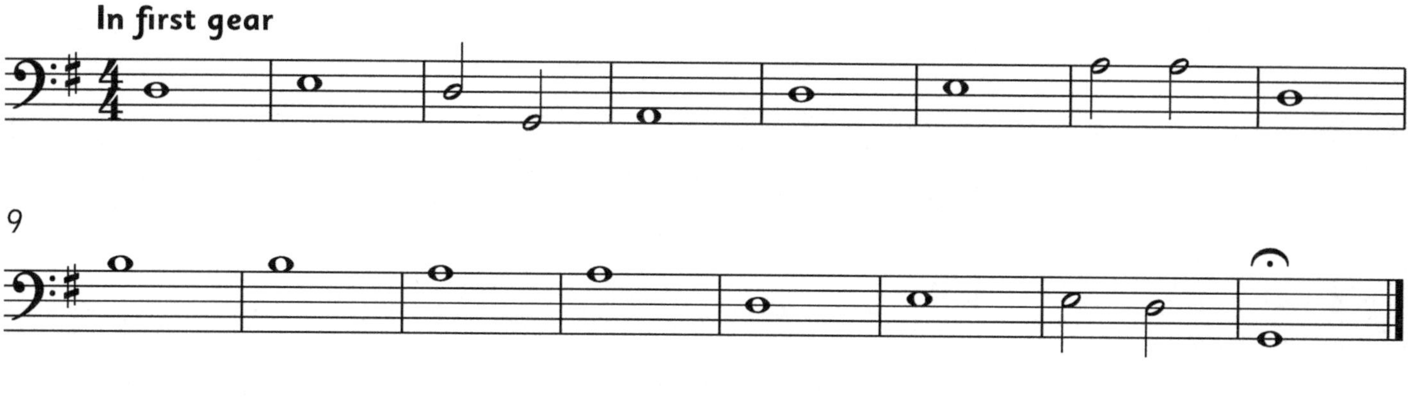

19. Tiptoe, boo!

Count 2 bars

KB & DB

Spookily

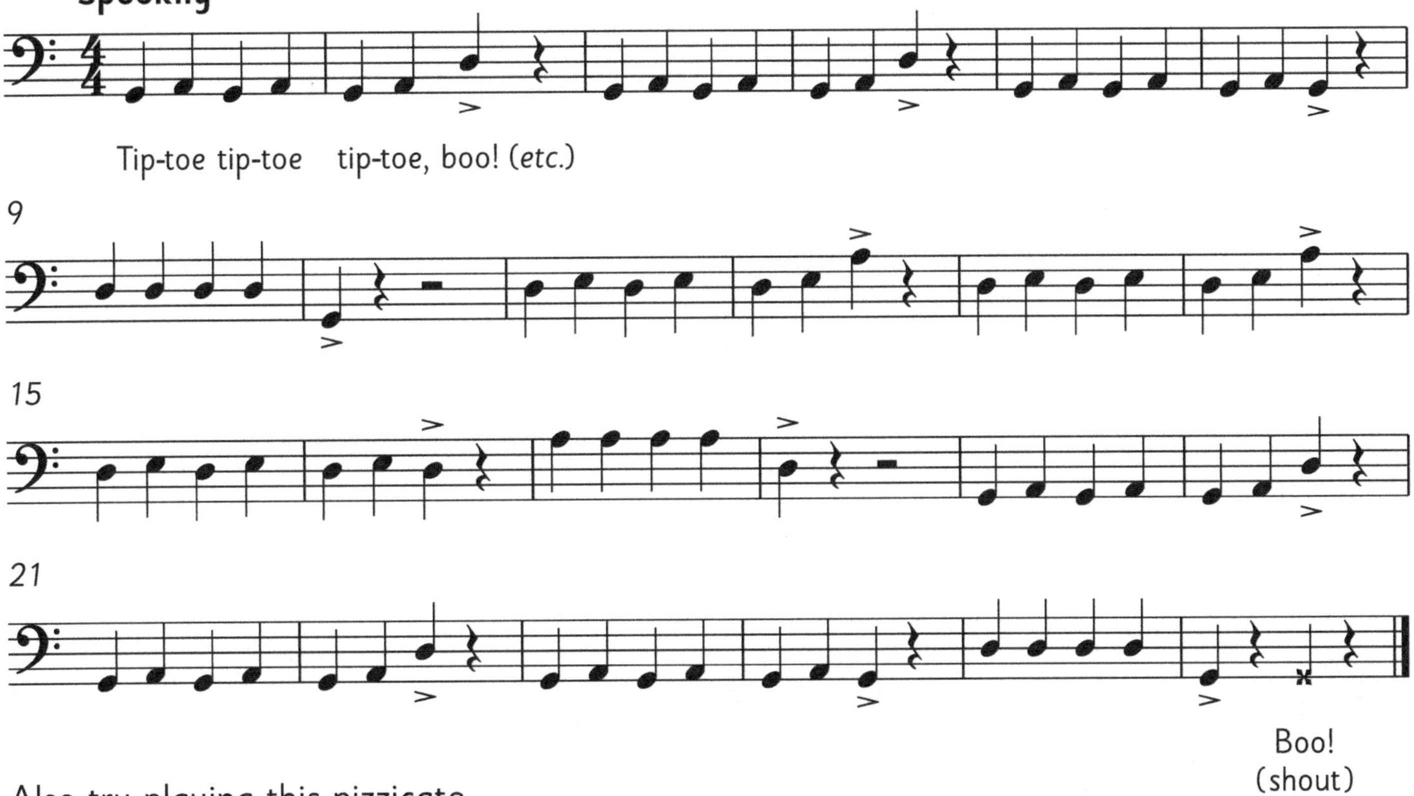

Also try playing this pizzicato.

20. Lazy cowboy

KB & DB

At a gentle trot

3rd Finger

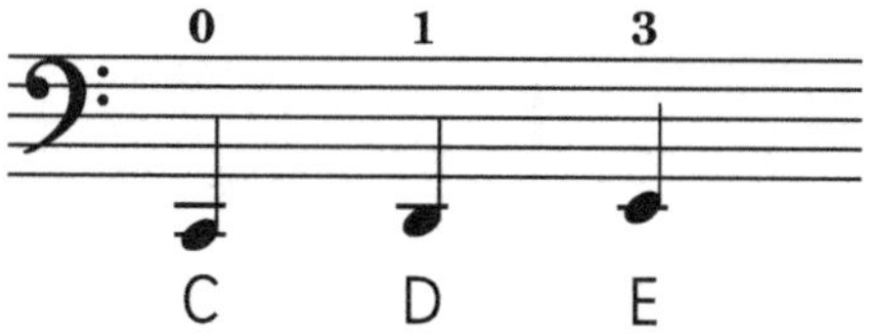

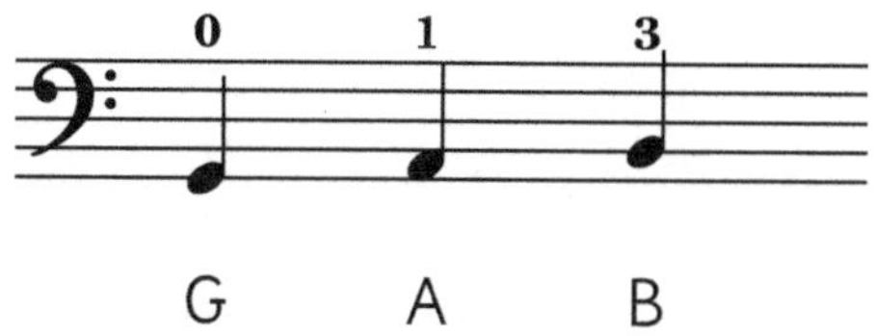

quavers
(eighth-notes)

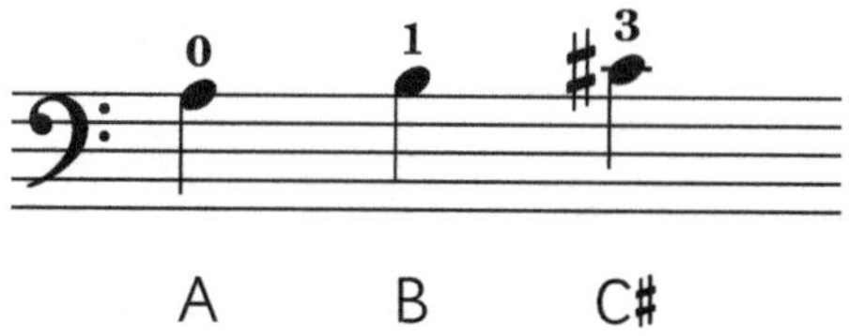

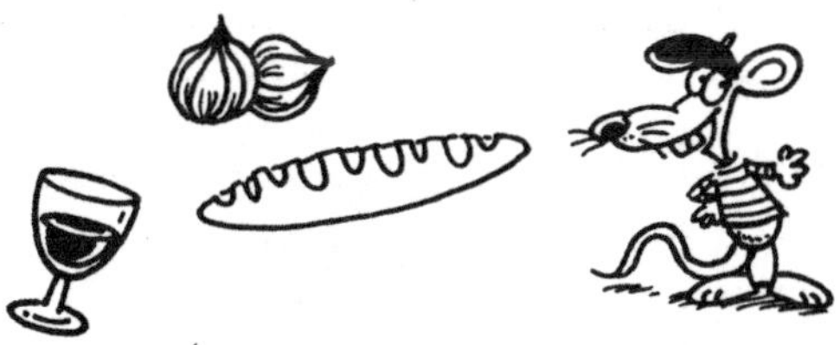

21. Off to Paris

French folk tune

22. City lights

KB & DB

23. Clare's song

Count 4 bars

KB & DB

When you can play slurs, come back and play this piece slurring three crotchets (quarter-notes) to a bow.

24. Phoebe in her petticoat

American folk tune

Swap parts when you do the repeat.

25. Peace garden

KB & DB

26. Summer sun

KB & DB

27. On the prowl

KB & DB

28. Knock, knock!

KB & DB

29. Ready, steady, go now!

KB & DB

30. Happy go lucky (for Iain)

Count 4 bars

KB & DB

Try the harder part of ‘Someone plucks, someone bows’ on page 3.

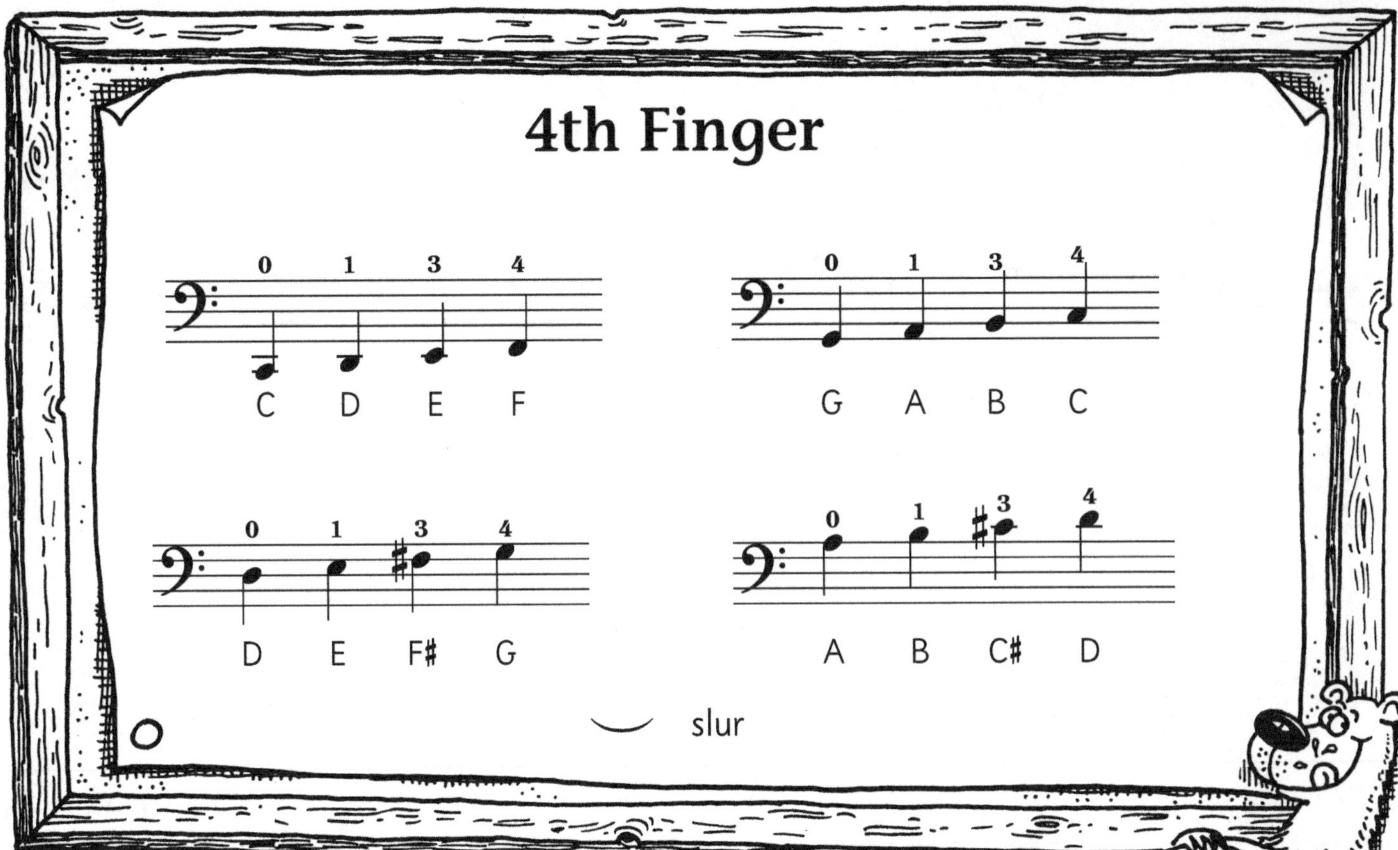

31. Algy met a bear

KB & DB
Words anon.

Swap parts when you do the repeat.

Try the harder part of 'Off to Paris' on page 14.

32. Listen to the rhythm

KB & DB

f
Lis - ten to the rhy - thm on my big cel - lo. Crot-chets sound like
Quar - ter - notes like
6
this: Crot-chets sound like that!
this: Quar - ter - notes like that!
11
Lis - ten to the rhy - thm on my big cel - lo. Mi - nims sound like
Half-notes sound like
16
this: Mi - nims sound like that!
this: Half-notes sound like that!
21
Lis - ten to the rhy - thm on my big cel - lo. Se - mi - breves like
Whole-notes sound like
26
this: Se - mi - breves like that!
this: Whole-notes sound like that!

33. Cattle ranch blues

KB & DB

Try the harder part of 'Hill an' gully rider' on page 4.

34. In the groove

Count 2 bars

KB & DB

35. Stamping dance

Czech folk tune

36. Walking bass

KB & DB

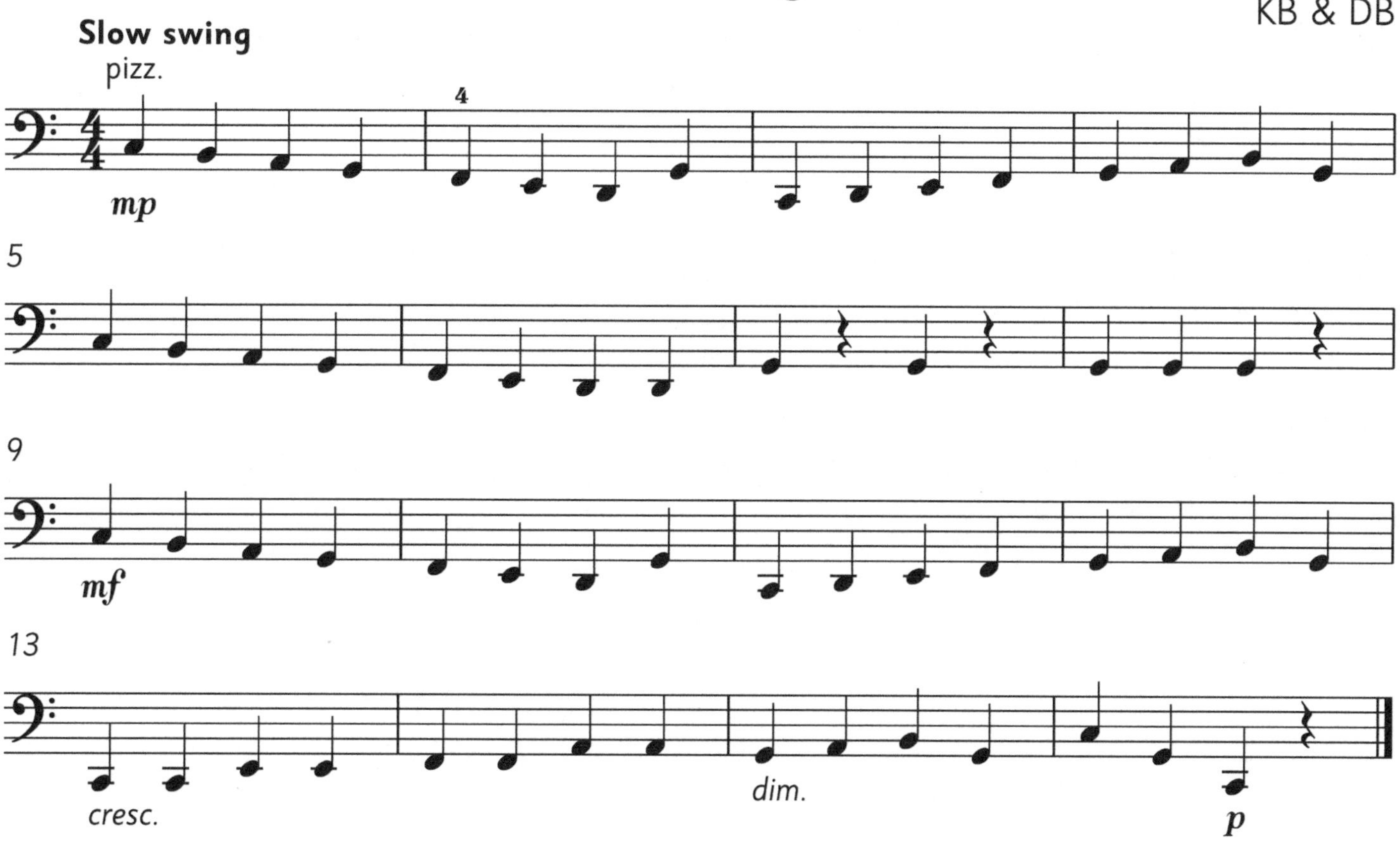

37. Chopsticks for two

KB & DB

38. Runaway train

Count 4 bars

KB & DB

Express train tempo

39. Distant bells

Count 2 bars

KB & DB

40. Lazy scale

KB & DB

41. The old castle

KB & DB

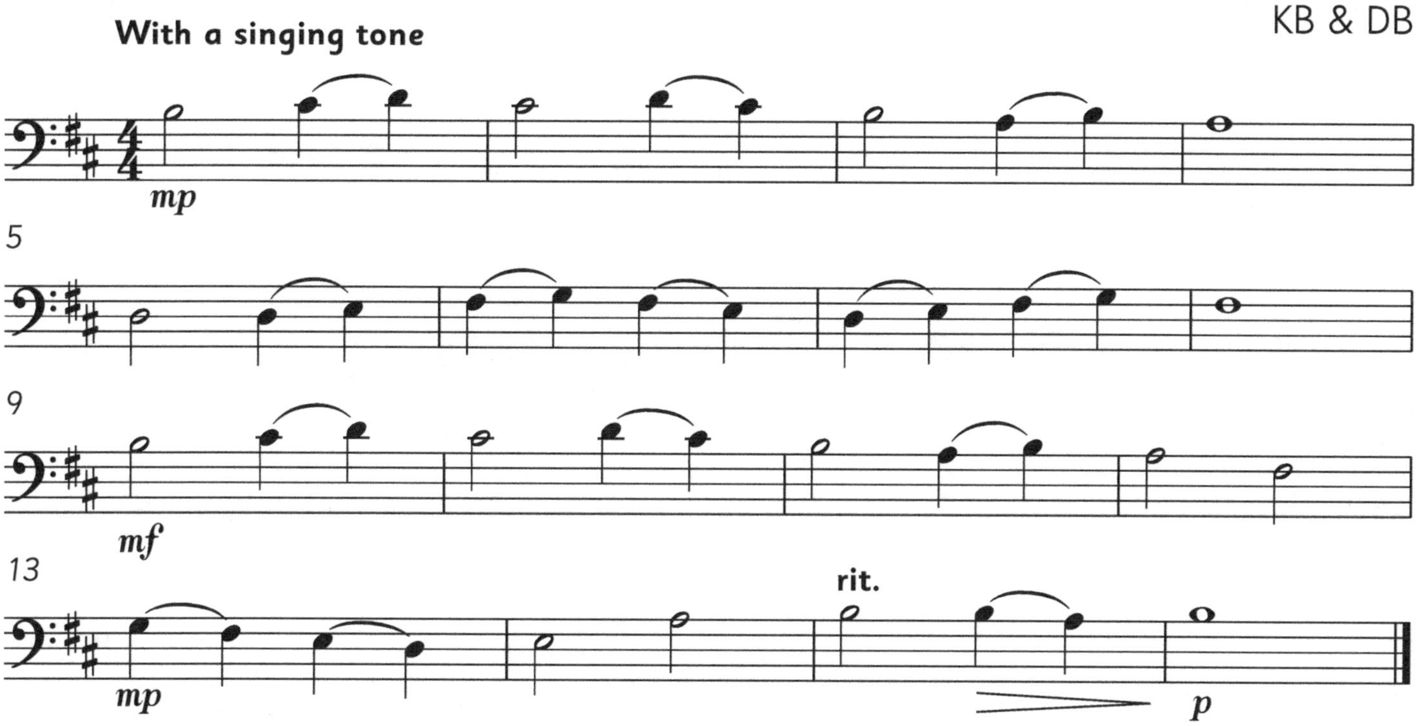

42. Rocking horse

Count 4 bars

KB & DB

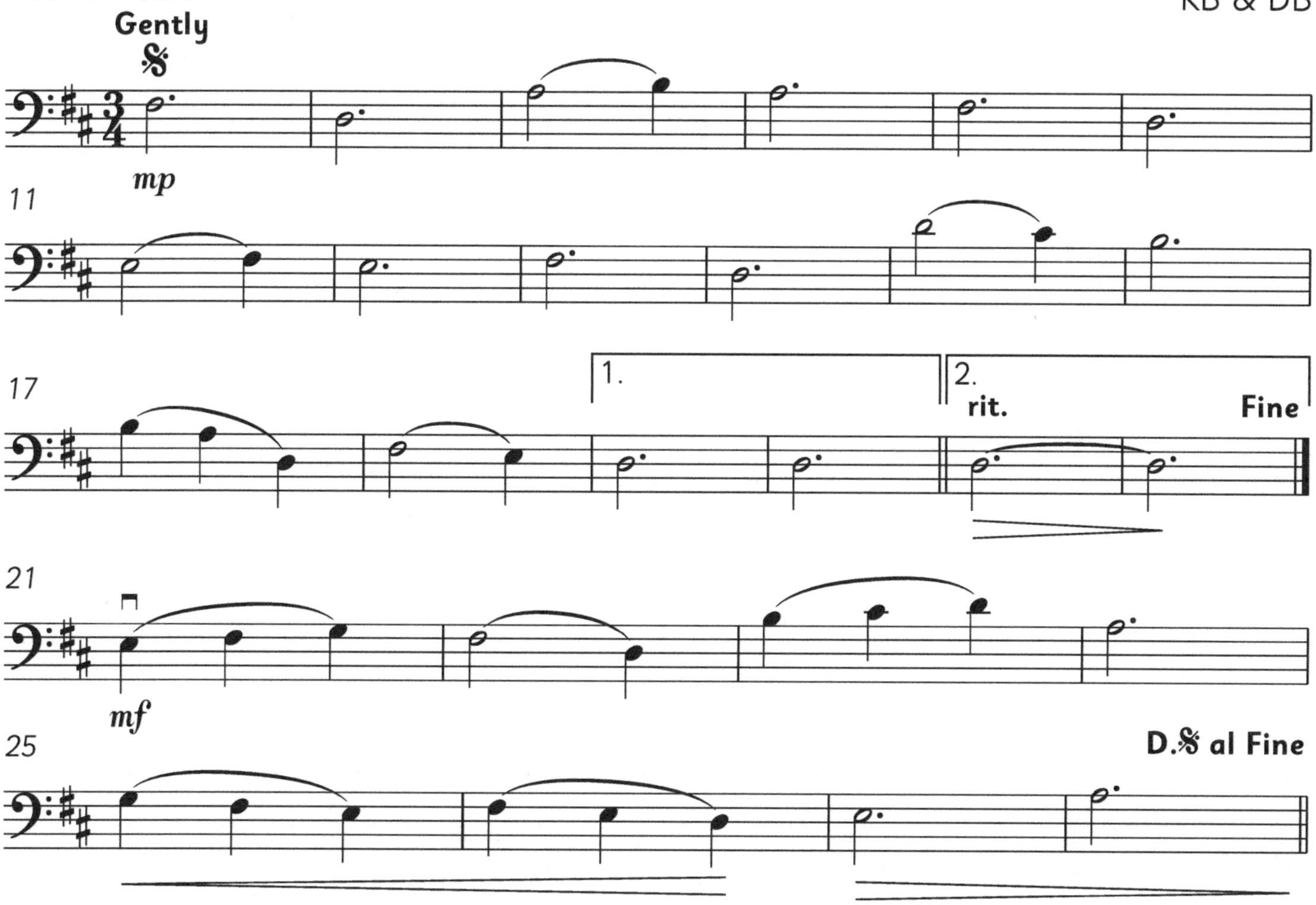

Try playing 'Clare's song' on page 15, slurring three crotchets (quarter-notes) to a bow.

43. Patrick's reel

Count 2 bars

KB & DB

Try the harder part of 'Ally bally' on page 11.

44. Calypso time

Count 2 bars

KB & DB

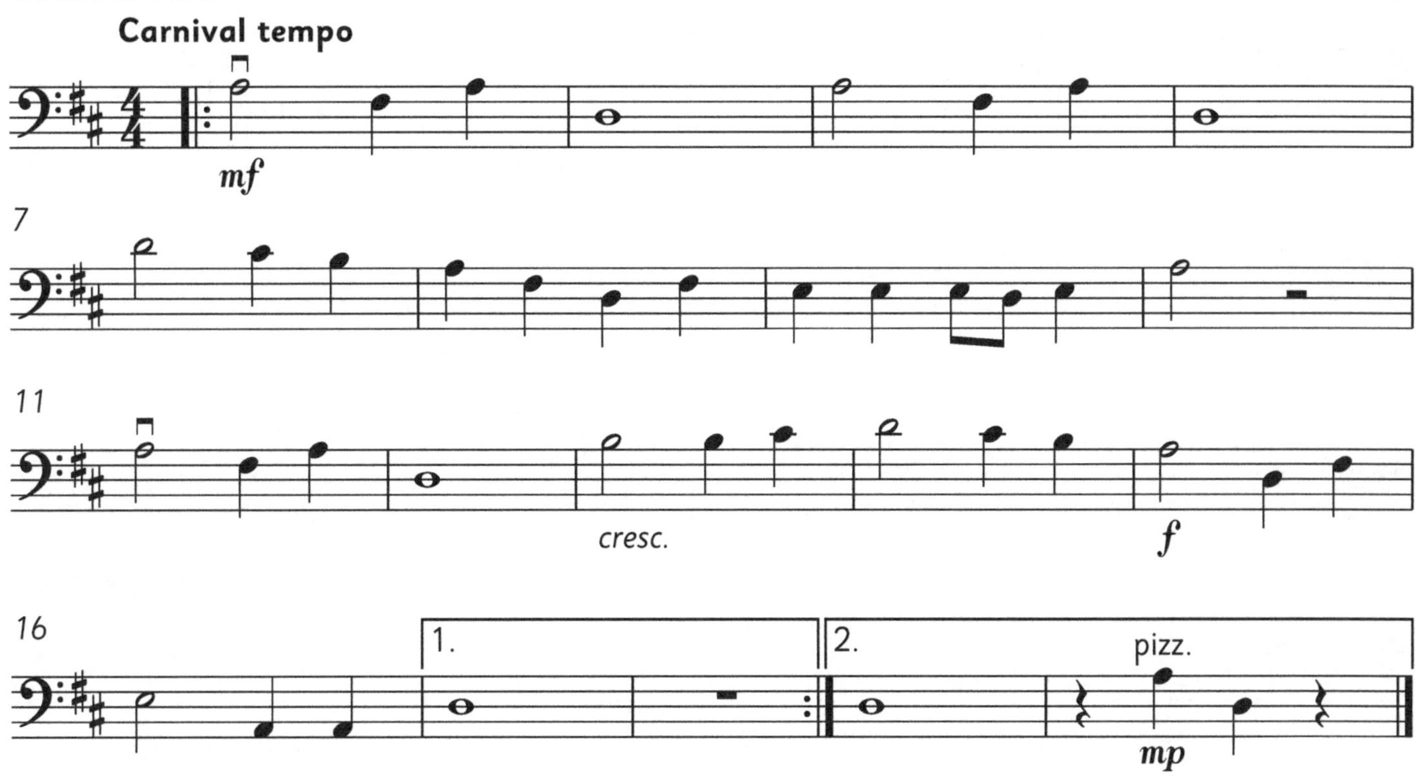

Try the harder part of 'Bow down, O Belinda' on page 2.

45. Cello Time

Count 4 bars

KB & DB

Scales and Scaley Things!

Playing scales and arpeggios with different rhythms is a great way to brighten up your practice.
Try each note of these scales and arpeggios with this rhythm:

Ready steady go now

Football teams, your friends' names, your favourite animals, and food can all be starting-points for your own rhythms. Make up some more patterns of your own.

G major scale

G major arpeggio

Add the arpeggio fingering like a telephone number below.

D major scale

D major arpeggio

C major scale

C major arpeggio

Super sprinter

KB & DB

Try sprinting with the metronome! Start in the slow lane with level 1 and work up to Olympic standard!

Level 1: steady ♩ = 60

Level 2: in training ♩ = 80

Level 3: Olympic standard ♩ = 100

Wave machine

KB & DB

Ring my number

KB & DB

* Use the empty boxes to write in the fingers needed to play these notes.

Challenge: can you play this tune starting on the G or the D string?

Music Fact-Finder Page

Here are some of the words and signs you will find in some of your pieces!

How to play it

pizzicato or pizz. = pluck
arco = with the bow
⊓ = down bow
V = up bow
> = accent
𝅗𝅥 with tremolo strokes = tremolo

Don't get lost!

𝄆 𝄇 = repeat marks

1. | 2. = first and second time bars
Play the first bar first time through; skip to the second bar on the repeat
D.C. al Fine = repeat from the beginning and stop at **Fine**
D.𝄋 al Fine = repeat from the sign 𝄋 and stop at **Fine**
rit. = gradually getting slower
a tempo = back to the first speed
𝄐 = pause

Volume control

p *(piano)* = quiet
mp *(mezzo-piano)* = moderately quiet
mf *(mezzo-forte)* = moderately loud
f *(forte)* = loud
ff *(fortissimo)* = very loud
𝆒 or *crescendo (cresc.)* = getting gradually louder
𝆓 or *diminuendo (dim.)* = getting gradually quieter